# CELEBRITY STORIES:
## TAYLOR SWIFT

Learn all about your favorite celebrity

JESS HOPE

_Celebrity Stories_

## Table of Contents

## Humble Beginnings and a Dream

In the quaint little town of Reading, Pennsylvania, on December 13, 1989, a future music icon was born. Her name was Taylor Alison Swift, and she would go on to become one of the most successful and influential artists of her generation.

Taylor's love for music started early. Her parents, Scott Kingsley Swift and Andrea Finlay, often played music around the house, exposing her to a wide variety of genres.

When Taylor was just nine years old, she began singing in a local karaoke competition circuit and quickly gained a reputation for her impressive vocal range and charismatic stage presence. It was then that she knew she wanted to pursue a career in music.

Taylor's parents were supportive of her dream, enrolling her in vocal and acting lessons. They even made the difficult decision to move the family to Hendersonville, Tennessee, so that Taylor could be closer to Nashville, the heart of the country music industry.

The move would prove to be a significant turning point in her life and career.

In Nashville, Taylor became a regular at the Bluebird Café, a famous songwriters' haven where many aspiring musicians showcased their talents in the hopes of being discovered. This was where Taylor's talent as a songwriter began to flourish. At the age of 12, she started learning to play the guitar, inspired by a computer repairman who showed her a few chords.

Before long, she was writing her own songs and performing them in front of audiences at the Bluebird and other local venues.

The road to success was not always smooth for Taylor. She faced her fair share of rejection and setbacks in her quest to make it in the music industry. In one notable incident, a music executive told the young singer-songwriter that she should be on a reality show instead of trying to make it in the music business.

But Taylor was not one to be deterred. She remained steadfast in her pursuit of her dreams, taking every opportunity to learn and grow as an artist.

Her hard work and determination eventually paid off. In 2004, Taylor caught the attention of Scott Borchetta, a music industry executive who was in the process of starting a new record label, Big Machine Records. Impressed by her talent and charisma, Borchetta signed the 15-year-old Taylor Swift to his fledgling label, setting the stage for her meteoric rise to fame.

Taylor's eponymous debut album, released in 2006, showcased her skills as a singer, songwriter, and storyteller. The album featured a mix of heartfelt ballads and catchy, up-tempo tracks, all penned by Taylor herself. The lead single, "Tim McGraw," was an ode to the country star and a love letter to high school romance. The song's poignant lyrics and infectious melody resonated with listeners and helped propel Taylor to the forefront of the country music scene.

As her music began to gain traction, so did her fanbase. Teenagers and young adults alike found comfort and inspiration in Taylor's honest and relatable lyrics. They saw themselves in her stories of love, heartbreak, and personal growth. With each new release, Taylor's popularity grew, and she soon became a household name.

However, Taylor's ambitions were not limited to the country music scene. She was determined to push the boundaries of her artistry and reach an even wider audience.

Her second album, "Fearless," released in 2008, marked the beginning of her foray into pop music. The record was a critical and commercial success, spawning several chart-topping hits, including "Love Story" and "You Belong with Me." It was during this time that Taylor also began to build her reputation as a live performer, captivating audiences with her "Fearless" not only solidified Taylor's status as a bona fide star but also earned her numerous accolades, including Album of the Year at the Grammy Awards, making her the youngest artist ever to win the prestigious honor at just 20 years old. The record-breaking success of "Fearless" was a testament to Taylor's ability to connect with her fans and capture the zeitgeist of her generation.

As Taylor continued to evolve as an artist, her music became increasingly more pop-oriented. Her third album, "Speak Now," released in 2010, was a self-penned confessional opus, showcasing her growth as a songwriter and her willingness to address personal experiences in her music.

The album, which included hits like "Mine" and "Back to December," further cemented her status as a crossover star, appealing to both country and pop music fans.

Throughout her career, Taylor has never shied away from reinventing herself. Her fourth album, "Red," released in 2012, saw her experimenting with various musical styles, incorporating elements of pop, rock, and electronic music.

The album featured the massive hit "We Are Never Ever Getting Back Together," which topped charts around the world and earned Taylor her first number-one song on the Billboard Hot 100.

Taylor's bold, chameleonic approach to her music would become a defining characteristic of her career, as demonstrated by her groundbreaking 2014 release, "1989." This album marked a significant departure from her country roots, embracing an unabashedly pop sound that showcased her versatility as an artist.

The record spawned multiple chart-topping hits, including "Shake It Off," "Blank Space," and "Bad Blood," and solidified her position as a global pop icon.

While Taylor's incredible success can be attributed to her talent, perseverance, and business acumen, her connection with her fans has always been at the heart of her meteoric rise. Her ability to cultivate a genuine bond with her audience, both through her music and her online presence, has set her apart from her contemporaries.

Taylor's legion of dedicated fans, affectionately known as "Swifties," have stood by her through every stage of her career, and their unwavering support has been a key factor in her enduring success.

In this book, we will delve deeper into the life and career of Taylor Swift, exploring the milestones and controversies that have shaped her journey from a starry-eyed teenager with a dream to one of the most successful and influential artists of her generation.

Through her ups and downs, her triumphs and heartaches, Taylor has remained a powerful symbol of resilience, creativity, and the unyielding power of a dream.

## The Art of Storytelling

Taylor's success as a songwriter can be largely attributed to her knack for weaving vivid narratives, capturing the essence of human emotions, and crafting relatable, heartfelt lyrics that resonate with her fans.

From a young age, Taylor was drawn to the magic of storytelling. Growing up, she would spend countless hours reading books and writing her own stories.

This love for storytelling would ultimately translate into her passion for songwriting, which she discovered at the age of 12.

One of the key aspects that set Taylor apart from her contemporaries is her focus on narrative-driven songs. While many pop artists rely on catchy hooks and danceable beats, Taylor's music often tells a story, taking the listener on a journey through her experiences, emotions, and observations.

Taylor's songwriting process is deeply personal, as she often draws from her own life for inspiration. By doing so, she creates a sense of intimacy with her listeners, allowing them to feel a genuine connection to her music. Fans find solace and comfort in her songs, recognizing their own experiences and emotions in her lyrics.

Throughout her career, Taylor has written songs that touch on a wide range of themes, from the innocence of first love to the pain of heartbreak, and from the joys of friendship to the challenges of personal growth.

One of her earliest hits, "Our Song," captures the sweetness of young love through a series of snapshots of everyday moments. In "Fifteen," Taylor reminisces about the trials and tribulations of high school, offering words of wisdom and encouragement to her younger fans.

As Taylor's career progressed, her songwriting continued to mature and evolve. Her later albums, such as "1989" and "Reputation," feature more introspective and reflective tracks that delve into her personal struggles and triumphs.

Songs like "Clean" and "Delicate" reveal a more vulnerable side of Taylor, as she navigates the complexities of love, fame, and self-discovery.

In addition to her autobiographical songs, Taylor has also demonstrated a remarkable ability to create fictional narratives that captivate her audience. One such example is "Love Story," a retelling of Shakespeare's Romeo and Juliet set to a modern, country-pop soundtrack.

The song's dramatic, star-crossed romance struck a chord with listeners, propelling it to the top of the charts and establishing Taylor as a masterful storyteller.

Taylor's storytelling prowess is not limited to her lyrics; she also extends her narratives through her music videos, live performances, and even her social media presence. Each of her music videos is a cinematic experience, often featuring elaborate sets, intricate costumes, and carefully crafted narratives that bring her songs to life.

Her live concerts are equally as immersive, incorporating theatrical elements that transport her audience into the world of her music.

By staying true to her storytelling roots, Taylor Swift has managed to create a body of work that transcends genres and speaks to the hearts of millions of fans around the world.

## The Musical Tapestry of Taylor Swift

Through her willingness to experiment with different genres, Taylor has created a rich tapestry of music that defies categorization and showcases her growth as an artist.

Growing up, Taylor was exposed to a wide array of musical genres, thanks to her parents' eclectic taste in music.

From classic rock bands like The Rolling Stones and The Beatles to legendary singer-songwriters like James Taylor and Joni Mitchell, these early influences played a significant role in shaping her own musical sensibilities. However, it was country music that ultimately captured her heart and laid the foundation for her career.

Country music was an integral part of Taylor's childhood, with artists such as Faith Hill, Shania Twain, and the Dixie Chicks featuring prominently in her family's music collection.

These artists not only inspired her love for the genre but also served as role models for her own career aspirations. As Taylor began to develop her own songwriting style, she incorporated elements of traditional country music, blending them with pop sensibilities to create a sound that was uniquely her own.

Throughout her career, Taylor has consistently demonstrated her willingness to experiment with different musical styles and genres.

Each of her albums has been marked by a distinct sound and aesthetic, showcasing her ability to reinvent herself while staying true to her roots as a storyteller. By incorporating elements of pop, rock, folk, electronic, and even hip-hop, Taylor has managed to transcend the confines of genre and create a musical landscape that is as diverse as it is compelling.

One of the most significant shifts in Taylor's sound occurred with the release of her 2012 album, "Red." While the album still featured country-inspired tracks like "Begin Again" and "All Too Well," it also included more pop and rock-leaning songs such as "We Are Never Ever Getting Back Together" and "I Knew You Were Trouble." This marked the beginning of Taylor's foray into pop music, a transition that would continue with her subsequent albums.

"1989," Taylor's fifth studio album, represented a complete departure from her country roots, embracing an unabashedly pop sound that was heavily influenced by the synth-pop and dance music of the 1980s. The album's infectious hooks, glossy production, and electronic beats demonstrated Taylor's versatility as an artist and cemented her status as a pop powerhouse. Notably, "1989" also marked the beginning of her collaboration with producer Max Martin, who would go on to play a significant role in shaping her sound in the years to come.

Taylor's exploration of different musical styles continued with "Reputation," her sixth studio album, which incorporated elements of hip-hop and electronic dance music. Working with producers like Jack Antonoff, Shellback, and Ali Payami, Taylor crafted a darker, edgier sound that reflected her evolving persona and the intense media scrutiny that she faced at the time. Songs like "Look What You Made Me Do" and "End Game" showcased her ability to adapt to new musical trends while maintaining her signature storytelling style.

Over the years, Taylor has also collaborated with a diverse array of artists from various genres, further expanding her musical horizons. From her duet with country legend Tim McGraw on "Highway Don't Care" to her collaboration with rapper Kendrick Lamar on "Bad Blood," these partnerships have allowed her to explore new sounds and styles while introducing her music to new audiences.

In 2020, Taylor surprised fans with the release of "Folklore," an album that marked yet another significant departure from her previous sound.

Produced in collaboration with The National's Aaron Dessner and her longtime collaborator Jack Antonoff, "Folklore" showcased a more stripped-down, introspective sound, heavily influenced by indie-folk and alternative music.

The album's dreamy, atmospheric production, coupled with Taylor's evocative storytelling, resonated with fans and critics alike, earning her widespread acclaim and several Grammy Awards, including Album of the Year.

The success of "Folklore" led to the release of its sister album, "Evermore," in December of the same year. Continuing in the same musical vein as its predecessor, "Evermore" further solidified Taylor's ability to reinvent herself and explore new sonic landscapes.

With collaborations featuring artists such as HAIM, Bon Iver, and The National, the album represented yet another milestone in her ever-evolving musical journey.

Taylor's willingness to experiment with different musical styles and genres is not only a testament to her versatility as an artist but also a reflection of her commitment to growth and evolution.

By constantly pushing the boundaries of her sound, she has created a rich and varied body of work that continues to captivate and inspire listeners around the world.

Aside from her musical influences and collaborations, Taylor's live performances have also played a crucial role in her career, allowing her to connect with her fans on a deeply personal level.

Known for her elaborate, theatrical concerts, Taylor has consistently raised the bar when it comes to live music, incorporating intricate set designs, choreography, and special effects to create a truly immersive experience for her audience.

Throughout her career, Taylor has embarked on several world tours, each more ambitious and spectacular than the last.

From the intimate, acoustic sets of her early days to the massive stadium shows of her later tours, Taylor's concerts are a testament to her growth as a performer and her unwavering dedication to her craft.

As one of the most successful recording artists in history, Taylor Swift has been no stranger to accolades and awards. With a career spanning over a decade, she has amassed numerous prestigious honors that recognize her musical accomplishments, her songwriting prowess, and her influence on popular culture.

Perhaps most notably, Taylor Swift is a multiple Grammy Award-winning artist, having won numerous awards across various categories. As of 2021, she had won 11 Grammy Awards, including three Album of the Year wins for her albums "Fearless," "1989," and "Folklore." With these achievements, Taylor became the first female artist and the youngest person ever to win the Album of the Year award twice, and she joined a select group of artists who have won the award three times.

In addition to her success at the Grammy Awards, Taylor has also been recognized with numerous American Music Awards (AMAs), Billboard Music Awards, and Country Music Association (CMA) Awards. Some of her most notable achievements include being named the AMA's Artist of the Year on three separate occasions, receiving the CMA's Pinnacle Award in recognition of her global impact on country music, and being honored with the Billboard Music Award for Top Female Artist multiple times.

Taylor's songwriting abilities have also been celebrated with various awards and honors. As mentioned in an earlier chapter, she has won the Nashville Songwriters Association International's Songwriter/Artist of the Year award seven times and has been honored with the Songwriters Hall of Fame's Hal David Starlight Award.

Beyond her musical accomplishments, Taylor Swift has also been recognized for her philanthropic efforts and her impact on popular culture.

In 2012, she received the Ripple of Hope Award from the Robert F. Kennedy Center for Justice and Human Rights for her commitment to social change. She was also honored with the Billboard Woman of the Year Award in 2014 and 2021, and in 2018, she was named one of TIME magazine's 100 Most Influential People.

## A Voice for Change – Advocacy and Philanthropy

From her support for various charitable causes to her outspoken stance on social and political issues, Taylor's dedication to making a difference is an integral part of her identity as an artist and a public figure.

Throughout her career, Taylor has been involved in numerous charitable endeavors, demonstrating a strong commitment to giving back to her community and supporting causes that are close to her heart. Early in her career, she established a pattern of donating proceeds from her music to charitable organizations. In 2007, she launched a campaign to protect children from online predators, donating proceeds from her single "Tied Together with a Smile" to the cause. This marked the beginning of her long-standing involvement in various charitable initiatives.

Education has always been a priority for Taylor, who has consistently supported initiatives aimed at improving access to quality education and empowering young people. In 2010, she donated $500,000 to help rebuild schools affected by flooding in Tennessee. She has also donated books to public libraries, provided funding for music education programs, and established the Taylor Swift Scholarship Fund to support aspiring musicians and artists.

In addition to her focus on education, Taylor has been a staunch advocate for disaster relief efforts. She has donated significant sums to the American Red Cross, as well as to organizations such as UNICEF and Save the Children, in response to various natural disasters around the world. Her contributions have helped provide essential aid to affected communities, demonstrating her unwavering commitment to making a tangible difference in the lives of those in need.

Taylor's philanthropy extends to a wide range of other causes, including healthcare, LGBTQ+ rights, and animal welfare. In 2012, she pledged $4 million to the Country Music Hall of Fame and Museum to fund the Taylor Swift Education Center, which aims to foster a love of music and the arts among children and young people. She has also supported organizations such as the Make-A-Wish Foundation, St. Jude Children's Research Hospital, and the Wounded Warrior Project.

As her career has progressed, Taylor has become increasingly vocal about social and political issues, using her platform to raise awareness and advocate for change. One of her most notable moments of activism came in 2018 when she broke her long-standing political silence to endorse Democratic candidates in the Tennessee midterm elections. In a heartfelt Instagram post, she urged her fans to register to vote and to support candidates who would fight for LGBTQ+ rights, racial equality, and women's rights. Her endorsement had a significant impact, with a surge in voter

registrations following her post.

Taylor's support for LGBTQ+ rights has been a consistent theme throughout her career. In 2019, she released the single "You Need to Calm Down," which served as an anthem for LGBTQ+ equality and a call to action for her fans to support the Equality Act, legislation aimed at preventing discrimination based on sexual orientation and gender identity.

She also made a substantial donation to the Tennessee Equality Project, an organization working to advance LGBTQ+ rights in her home state.

In recent years, Taylor has become a powerful advocate for women's rights and gender equality, using her platform to amplify the voices of survivors and to call for change within the music industry and society at large. In 2017, she won a symbolic $1 in a sexual assault lawsuit, sending a powerful message about the importance of holding perpetrators accountable and supporting survivors.

She has also spoken out about her experiences with sexism in the music industry, highlighting the double standards and unfair expectations faced by female artists.

Through her advocacy and philanthropy, Taylor Swift has made a lasting impact on countless lives and demonstrated the power of using one's platform for positive change. Her commitment to various causes reflects her deep-rooted belief in the importance of giving back and making a difference in the world.

In addition to her activism and philanthropy, Taylor has also been a trailblazer within the music industry, challenging the status quo and advocating for artists' rights. One of her most notable achievements in this regard came in 2015 when she wrote an open letter to Apple, criticizing the company's initial decision not to pay artists during the free trial period of their streaming service, Apple Music. In response to her letter, Apple reversed its decision, marking a significant victory for musicians and highlighting Taylor's influence within the industry.

Taylor's battle for artists' rights continued in 2019 when she publicly called out talent manager Scooter Braun and her former record label, Big Machine Label Group, over the ownership of her master recordings. The highly publicized dispute brought attention to the issue of artists' rights and control over their creative output, sparking a broader conversation about the power dynamics within the music industry.

Throughout her career, Taylor has consistently pushed for fair compensation and greater creative control for artists, advocating for changes within the industry that prioritize the rights and well-being of creators. Her efforts have not only improved her own circumstances but have also paved the way for other artists to assert their rights and demand fair treatment.

As we have explored in this chapter, Taylor Swift's advocacy, philanthropy, and commitment to social change are essential components of her identity as an artist and a public figure. Her willingness to use her platform to raise awareness, support important causes, and fight for change demonstrates her dedication to making the world a better place, both through her music and her actions.

## Lights, Camera, Action – Taylor Swift's Filmography

Although best known for her musical accomplishments, Taylor has demonstrated a passion for acting and has made several noteworthy contributions to the visual medium, showcasing her versatility as an artist and entertainer.

Taylor Swift's first venture into acting came in 2009 when she appeared in an episode of the popular crime drama "CSI: Crime Scene Investigation." In the episode titled "Turn, Turn, Turn," Taylor played the role of troubled teenager Haley Jones. Although this was only a guest appearance, it marked the beginning of her journey into the world of acting and revealed her interest in exploring different facets of her creativity.

In 2010, Taylor made her big-screen debut in the ensemble romantic comedy "Valentine's Day," directed by Garry Marshall. She played the role of Felicia, a high school student who is romantically involved with a character played by Taylor Lautner. While the film received mixed reviews from critics, it was a commercial success and offered Taylor an opportunity to showcase her acting abilities in a lighthearted context.

Continuing to explore her passion for acting, Taylor lent her voice to the character of Audrey in the 2012 animated film "The Lorax," based on the beloved children's book by Dr. Seuss. As Audrey, Taylor brought warmth and depth to the role, and the film was both a critical and commercial success.

In 2014, Taylor made a memorable cameo in the dystopian action film "The Giver," based on the novel by Lois Lowry.

Playing the character Rosemary, a previous Receiver of Memory who met a tragic end, Taylor's haunting performance added emotional weight to the film and showcased her ability to take on more dramatic roles.

Perhaps one of Taylor's most significant contributions to film was her role in the 2019 movie adaptation of the hit Broadway musical "Cats," directed by Tom Hooper. Portraying the character Bombalurina, Taylor not only acted but also co-wrote the original song "Beautiful Ghosts" with legendary composer Andrew Lloyd Webber.

Although the film itself received mixed-to-negative reviews, Taylor's performance and songwriting were praised by many critics.

Beyond her roles in feature films, Taylor Swift has also been the subject of two documentaries that offer a glimpse into her life and creative process.

The first, "Taylor Swift: Journey to Fearless," was released in 2010 and chronicled her rise to fame and the creation of her Fearless Tour.

The second documentary, "Miss Americana," premiered at the Sundance Film Festival in 2020 and provided an intimate look at Taylor's life, career, and personal struggles, as well as her growth as an artist and activist.

In addition to her film and television appearances, Taylor has also made her mark on the visual medium through her iconic music videos.

Often serving as a co-director and collaborating with renowned filmmakers such as Joseph Kahn and Drew Kirsch, Taylor has created a series of visually stunning, narrative-driven videos that showcase her creativity and storytelling abilities. Some of her most memorable music videos include "Blank Space," "Bad Blood," "Look What You Made Me Do," and "The Man."

As Taylor Swift continues to make her mark on the world of film and television, it is exciting to consider what future projects she may undertake. Given her track record of pushing boundaries and challenging herself as an artist, it is not hard to imagine her taking on more substantial roles, exploring new genres, or even stepping behind the camera to direct her own projects.

In the meantime, her existing body of film and television work stands as a testament to her versatility and her willingness to embrace new challenges.

Taylor Swift's filmography, while still a relatively small part of her overall artistic output, adds another layer to her already impressive legacy, and it will be fascinating to see how this aspect of her career continues to unfold in the years to come.

## A Business Savvy Superstar – Taylor Swift's Entrepreneurial Pursuits

In this chapter, we will delve into Taylor Swift's ventures as an entrepreneur, examining her various business endeavors, partnerships, and the ways in which she has leveraged her personal brand to create a successful and diverse range of enterprises.

As one of the most influential and powerful figures in the entertainment industry, Taylor has demonstrated remarkable business acumen and an ability to adapt to the ever-changing landscape of the music business.

Taylor Swift's entrepreneurial journey began early in her career when she signed with Big Machine Records, an independent label founded by Scott Borchetta.

At the time, Taylor was only 15 years old, and her decision to join an independent label rather than a major record company allowed her more creative control and a greater share of the profits from her music. This early decision would prove to be a pivotal moment in her career, setting the stage for a series of entrepreneurial endeavors that would come to define her as not just a talented musician, but also a savvy businesswoman.

One of the most significant aspects of Taylor Swift's entrepreneurship is her ability to cultivate and maintain a strong personal brand.

Through her music, her public persona, and her carefully curated social media presence, Taylor has created a unique and authentic identity that resonates deeply with her fans. This personal brand has become a valuable asset that Taylor has been able to leverage in various business ventures, partnerships, and endorsements.

Throughout her career, Taylor has been involved in numerous brand partnerships and endorsement deals that have not only generated significant revenue but have also allowed her to maintain control over her image and creative output.

Some of her most notable partnerships include deals with major brands such as Keds, Diet Coke, Apple Music, and AT&T.

In each of these partnerships, Taylor has been able to align her personal brand with the values and aesthetics of the companies she works with, ensuring that these collaborations are both financially rewarding and artistically fulfilling.

In addition to her endorsement deals and partnerships, Taylor Swift has also ventured into the world of merchandise and retail, creating a vast array of products that allow her fans to engage with her brand on a deeper level.

From clothing and accessories to fragrance lines and limited-edition collaborations with various artists and designers, Taylor's merchandise offerings have become an essential part of her entrepreneurial portfolio. By creating high-quality, unique products that reflect her personal style and artistic vision, Taylor has been able to generate significant revenue while also providing her fans with a tangible connection to her world.

Another key component of Taylor Swift's entrepreneurship is her involvement in the management and production aspects of her music and live performances. Taylor has consistently played an active role in the creative and business decisions surrounding her albums, tours, and music videos, ensuring that her artistic vision is always at the forefront. This hands-on approach has not only allowed her to maintain control over her work but has also given her valuable experience and insight into the inner workings of the music industry.

In recent years, Taylor has also been a vocal advocate for artists' rights and fair compensation in the digital age. Her decision to remove her music from Spotify in 2014, due to concerns over the streaming platform's royalty payment structure, made headlines and sparked a broader conversation about the value of music in the digital era. In 2015, Taylor penned an open letter to Apple Music, criticizing the company's decision not to pay royalties to artists during the platform's free trial period. In response, Apple quickly changed its policy, demonstrating Taylor's ability to effect meaningful

change within the industry. These actions, coupled with her ongoing commitment to advocating for artists' rights, have solidified her status as a powerful force within the music business.

As Taylor Swift's career has progressed, so too has her entrepreneurial spirit. In 2019, she made the bold decision to leave Big Machine Records and sign with Republic Records and Universal Music Group.

As part of her new deal, Taylor negotiated for more favorable terms, including retaining ownership of her future master recordings – a significant move in an industry where artists often relinquish control over their work. This decision not only demonstrated her business acumen but also served as a powerful example for other artists seeking to maintain control over their careers and creative output.

In 2021, Taylor embarked on an ambitious project to re-record her earlier albums in response to the controversial sale of her original master recordings. This undertaking, dubbed the "Taylor's Version" project, has not only allowed her to regain control over her music but has also provided her with an opportunity to revisit and reimagine her past work. By re-recording her music, Taylor has turned a challenging situation into a creative and entrepreneurial triumph, showcasing her resilience and adaptability as both an artist and a businesswoman.

Beyond her music-related ventures, Taylor Swift has also demonstrated an interest in exploring other areas of the entertainment industry. As discussed in a previous chapter, she has dabbled in acting, appearing in television shows and movies, and lending her voice to animated films. While her acting career is still in its early stages, these ventures reveal her willingness to take risks, expand her horizons, and explore new creative avenues – all essential qualities of a successful entrepreneur.

## The Magic of the Stage – Taylor Swift's Phenomenal Live Tours

From her early days as an opening act to her record-breaking stadium tours, Taylor's live performances have evolved into immersive, theatrical experiences that have not only entertained millions of fans but also cemented her status as one of the most powerful live performers of her generation.

## Taylor Swift's Fearless Tour (2009-2010)

Taylor Swift's first headlining tour, the Fearless Tour, marked the beginning of her meteoric rise to touring stardom. Kicking off in April 2009, the tour supported her second studio album, "Fearless," which was released in 2008. The Fearless Tour spanned 13 months and consisted of 118 shows across North America, Europe, and Australia. With an estimated attendance of over 1.1 million people, the tour grossed more than $66 million, establishing Taylor as a major touring force in the music industry.

The Fearless Tour was notable for its elaborate stage design, which included a multi-level castle set, numerous costume changes, and elaborate choreography. Taylor's penchant for storytelling and her ability to connect with her audience were on full display during the tour, as she performed fan-favorite songs like "Love Story," "You Belong with Me," and "Fifteen."

**Speak Now World Tour (2011-2012)**

Following the success of her Fearless Tour, Taylor embarked on her second headlining tour, the Speak Now World Tour, in support of her third studio album, "Speak Now." The tour began in February 2011 and concluded in March 2012, encompassing a total of 110 shows across North America, Europe, Asia, and Australia. The Speak Now World Tour boasted a larger stage production than its predecessor, featuring a dramatic, gothic-inspired set design, numerous costume changes, and even aerial acrobatics.

The tour attracted over 1.6 million fans and grossed more than $123 million, further solidifying Taylor's status as a global touring phenomenon. Memorable performances from the Speak Now World Tour include hits like "Mine," "Back to December," and "Enchanted."

**The Red Tour (2013-2014)**

Taylor's fourth studio album, "Red," served as the foundation for her third headlining tour, the Red Tour.

Kicking off in March 2013, the tour spanned 15 months and included 86 shows across North America, Europe, Asia, and Oceania. With an estimated attendance of over 1.7 million people, the Red Tour grossed more than $150 million.

The Red Tour featured an even more elaborate stage production than previous tours, with a multi-level stage, numerous costume changes, and a variety of special effects.

The setlist included popular tracks from the "Red" album, such as "We Are Never Ever Getting Back Together," "I Knew You Were Trouble," and "22," as well as a selection of songs from Taylor's earlier albums.

## The 1989 World Tour (2015)

Taylor Swift's fifth studio album, "1989," marked a significant shift in her musical direction, moving away from her country roots and embracing a more pop-oriented sound.

The 1989 World Tour was launched in support of the album, beginning in May 2015 and concluding in December of the same year. The tour comprised 85 shows across North America, Europe, Asia, and Australia.

The 1989 World Tour was a massive success, attracting over 2.2 million fans and grossing more than $250 million, making it one of the highest-grossing tours of all time.

The tour's stage production was more ambitious than ever before, featuring a custom-built, 110-foot-long stage with a 360-degree rotating platform, elaborate video projections, and a host of special effects.

Throughout the tour, Taylor invited numerous special guests to join her on stage, ranging from fellow musicians to actors and athletes.

These surprise appearances added an element of excitement and unpredictability to each show and further solidified Taylor's reputation as a consummate performer. Memorable performances from the 1989 World Tour include hits like "Shake It Off," "Blank Space," and "Bad Blood."

**Reputation Stadium Tour (2018)**

Following the release of her sixth studio album, "Reputation," Taylor embarked on her fifth headlining tour and her first all-stadium tour, aptly named the Reputation Stadium Tour.

The tour kicked off in May 2018 and concluded in November of the same year, consisting of 53 shows across North America, Europe, Asia, and Australia.

The Reputation Stadium Tour was a massive undertaking, featuring a colossal, 110-foot-tall stage, three smaller stages spread throughout the stadium, and a host of cutting-edge special effects, including pyrotechnics, aerial stunts, and giant inflatable snakes.

The tour attracted over 2.8 million fans and grossed more than $345 million, breaking the record for the highest-grossing tour in U.S. history, previously held by The Rolling Stones.

In addition to performing hits from the "Reputation" album, such as "Look What You Made Me Do," "End Game," and "Delicate," Taylor also treated fans to a selection of songs from her earlier albums, reimagined with fresh arrangements and visual elements.

## Lover Fest (2020 - Postponed)

In support of her seventh studio album, "Lover," Taylor Swift initially announced a series of festival-style performances called Lover Fest, scheduled for 2020. The events were set to take place in various cities across the United States and Europe, with Taylor headlining each show. However, due to the COVID-19 pandemic, Lover Fest was postponed indefinitely, leaving fans eagerly anticipating Taylor's eventual return to the stage.

Throughout her career, Taylor Swift's live tours have been an essential component of her success and her connection with her fans. From the early days of the Fearless Tour to the record-breaking Reputation Stadium Tour, Taylor has consistently pushed the boundaries of live performance, creating unforgettable experiences for millions of fans around the world.

As she continues to evolve and grow as an artist, there is no doubt that her future tours will be marked by the same innovation, creativity, and passion that have come to define her incredible live shows. With each new album and tour, Taylor Swift cements her legacy as one of the most powerful and captivating live performers of her generation.

## Legacy – The Lasting Impact of Taylor Swift

From her record-breaking success and iconic performances to her role as a trailblazer and advocate for change, Taylor's enduring influence is a testament to her incredible talent, relentless work ethic, and unwavering commitment to her artistry.

Taylor Swift's meteoric rise to fame and her enduring success can be attributed to a combination of her exceptional songwriting abilities, her captivating storytelling, her versatile musical style, and her genuine connection with her fans. Over the years, she has become a global superstar, breaking records and garnering accolades that place her among the most iconic and influential artists of her generation.

One of the most remarkable aspects of Taylor's career is her consistent chart-topping success.

With numerous multi-platinum albums and countless hit singles, she has solidified her status as a music industry powerhouse. As of the time of writing, she has amassed 11 Grammy Awards, including three Album of the Year wins, a feat achieved by only a handful of artists in history. She has also sold over 200 million albums worldwide, making her one of the best-selling music artists of all time.

In addition to her commercial success, Taylor has also received widespread critical acclaim for her work, with many praising her ability to craft poignant, emotionally resonant songs that capture the complexity and nuance of human experience. Her albums, from her eponymous debut to her more recent releases like "Folklore" and "Evermore," have been met with rave reviews, further solidifying her reputation as a consummate artist and storyteller.

Throughout her career, Taylor has also been a trailblazer in the music industry, pushing boundaries and challenging conventions in a variety of ways. As a young female artist who emerged in the predominantly male-dominated country music scene, she defied expectations and carved out a space for herself, ultimately transcending the confines of genre to create a sound that was uniquely her own.

Taylor's willingness to experiment with different musical styles and to continually evolve as an artist has set her apart from her contemporaries and earned her a reputation as a fearless innovator. By constantly reinventing herself and exploring new creative avenues, she has managed to stay relevant and maintain her appeal to a diverse and ever-expanding fan base.

Beyond her music, Taylor's influence extends to her live performances, which have consistently set the bar for what a concert experience can be. From her intimate, acoustic shows in her early days to her elaborate, stadium-filling spectacles in more recent years, Taylor's concerts have evolved into immersive, theatrical experiences that transport her fans into the world of her music. These performances, marked by intricate set designs, choreography, and special effects, have become iconic in their own right, further cementing her status as a legendary performer.

Taylor's impact on the music industry is not limited to her artistry, as she has also used her platform to advocate for change and to fight for the rights of her fellow musicians. As discussed in the previous chapter, her efforts to challenge the status quo and to promote fair compensation and creative control for artists have had a profound effect on the industry, paving the way for other artists to assert their rights and demand fair treatment.

Outside of the music industry, Taylor has also made a significant impact through her advocacy and philanthropy, using her platform to raise awareness and support for a variety of important causes. As detailed in Chapter 4, her commitment to making a difference in the world is an integral part of her identity as a public figure, and her efforts to effect positive change have inspired countless others to follow in her footsteps.

Furthermore, Taylor's role as a role model for young people cannot be understated.

Throughout her career, she has consistently demonstrated the importance of hard work, resilience, and staying true to oneself, serving as a powerful example of what can be achieved through dedication and perseverance. Her relatable songwriting and honest, open approach to her life and experiences have allowed her fans to see themselves in her music, fostering a sense of connection and understanding that transcends age, gender, and cultural boundaries.

The influence of Taylor Swift can also be seen in the ways she has inspired the next generation of musicians and artists. Her success as a songwriter, performer, and advocate for change has paved the way for other young artists to pursue their dreams and challenge the status quo, creating a lasting impact on the music industry and popular culture as a whole.

As we reflect on the incredible career of Taylor Swift, it is clear that her legacy is multifaceted and far-reaching.

Her contributions to music, her advocacy for change, and her ability to connect with fans around the world have made her an enduring symbol of resilience, creativity, and the power of dreaming big. As she continues to write her own story, one can only imagine the heights she will continue to reach and the indelible mark she will continue to leave on the world.

Taylor Swift's life and career serve as a testament to the power of talent, hard work, and determination.

Her journey from a young girl with a guitar and a dream to a global superstar and a force for change is an inspiring story that will continue to resonate with fans and admirers for generations to come. As we look to the future, there is no doubt that Taylor Swift's legacy will continue to grow and evolve, reflecting the enduring impact of her artistry, her activism, and her unwavering commitment to making the world a better place through her music and her actions.

## What Did You Think?

Thank you so much for choosing and reading this book about the inspiring life and career of Taylor Swift. We know you have countless options when it comes to selecting reading material, and we are truly grateful that you have decided to spend your valuable time delving into the journey of this extraordinary artist.

Throughout the pages of this book, we have aimed to provide you with an in-depth exploration of Taylor's remarkable accomplishments, her undeniable talent, and her unwavering dedication to her craft. We hope that you have not only enjoyed this journey but also found inspiration and appreciation for the hard work, resilience, and passion that have propelled Taylor Swift to the pinnacle of the music industry.

Once again, thank you for choosing this book and for taking the time to immerse yourself in the fascinating world of Taylor Swift. We genuinely appreciate your support and enthusiasm, and we hope that you continue to find inspiration, joy, and connection in the incredible music and story of this truly remarkable artist.

With heartfelt gratitude,
Jess x

Made in United States
North Haven, CT
29 October 2023